W9-CKH-425

Stella Robinson

Textiles

Illustrated by Derek Lucas

The Bookwright Press
New York • 1984

Endeavor Books

Initiated and edited by Stella Robinson, the books in the
Endeavor series have been researched and written by
qualified scientists and engineers, and each title covers one
aspect of our scientific and technological development.

With the help of biographical notes, full color illustrations
and explanatory diagrams, each book highlights the major
personalities, discoveries and developments in a particular
field of scientific or technological progress.

Ranging in scope from earliest times to the present day, the
series provides a comprehensive account of the struggle to
understand the natural world and organize the
environment to our benefit.

Other titles in the series

Health and Medicine
Tools and Manufacture

First published in the United States in 1984 by
The Bookwright Press, 387 Park Avenue South, New York, NY 10016

First published in 1983 by Wayland Publishers Limited
49 Lansdowne Place, Brighton, East Sussex BN3 H1F, England

© Copyright 1983 Design Practitioners
All rights reserved

ISBN 531-04784-9

Library of Congress Catalog Card Number 83-72802
Printed in Italy by G. Canale & C.S.p.A., Turin

Contents

Cover picture – Hargreaves Spinning Jenny. This is a slightly modified jenny with a vertical driving wheel; his original model had an almost horizontal wheel. (Page 24)

Title page – An upright loom in use in Africa today. It is much the same as the first vertical looms which were invented 4000 years ago.

A dropped spindle.

The history of textiles

What are textiles, and why have they played such an important part in the history of the last 7,000 years? This book looks at these questions and describes the changing ways that textiles have been produced over the centuries.

Textiles are materials or *fabrics* that are made by *spinning* and *weaving*. Clothes, blankets, curtains, carpets and coverings, like many other household articles are made from textiles, but of all these, clothes are the most important. In colder climates, clothing is not only necessary for comfort, but is essential for survival.

Nobody knows when men and women lost the "fur" on their bodies, but when they did they must have been living in a warm climate where food was plentiful all year round. More than a million years ago our earliest ancestors must have lived rather as the chimpanzee does today, feeding on leaves and fruit, with an occasional meal of meat.

Humans, as they evolved, developed differently from the chimpanzees and other apes. Apart from losing the hair on their bodies, they learned to communicate by speech, and they could stand upright, thus freeing their hands to make and use simple tools.

With the first primitive tools, made by chipping and shaping stones, they could kill and skin large animals, and about three million years ago they became what is known as "hunter-gatherers." This means that for the first time men could hunt for food, and not rely on "scavenging" (eating the meat killed by other animals) for their meat. The skins of the animals could be used to keep warm, so people were able to live in the many cooler areas of the earth.

Stone Age.

Greek – 500 BC.

Norman – 11th Century.

Elizabethan – 16th Century.

4

About 10,000 years ago, people first learned how to make pottery and baskets. Later they discovered how to spin and weave cloth.

Methods of textile production have changed over the ages, as new ideas have arisen, and new discoveries have been made. In the modern world the need for attractive, comfortable and cheap clothing is so great that modern machinery alone can cope with the demand.

Many of the old machines, often impressive and beautiful, can now be found in museums, but even today the most ancient methods of production are still in use in the less developed areas of the world.

Many other old fashioned techniques are in use in the West also – but not for the purposes of serious production! Increasingly the handicrafts of spinning and weaving are being revived, for pleasure, as more and more people discover the interest and enjoyment of making textiles in the traditional way.

Clothing has other functions as well. Clothes help describe people's personalities and jobs – people "dress up" for important occasions like weddings and parties, and wear certain clothes like scarves or hats to show their support for a particular team. And lots of people such as school children, soldiers, policemen, churchmen, and judges wear special clothes, or uniforms, to show they belong to a particular organization or do particular jobs.

How clothes have changed through the ages: the wealthy, until the present day, have always been conspicuous by the clothes they wear. Keeping up with the fashion may sometimes have been very uncomfortable!

Regency – early 19th Century.

Victorian – 19th Century.

1920's.

Present day.

The First Textiles

The earliest attempts by men and women to produce textiles must have been dependent on the plants and animals they found in their natural environment.

The first knowledge of the weaving process probably came about when people learned to make baskets from reeds and grasses by interweaving bundles of leaves in and out of upright sticks. With the same material they could make mats by "darning" the leaves.

The principle of *spinning* could have been learned when they first made ropes. In mat- or basket-making the leaves can lie parallel and are easily pulled apart.

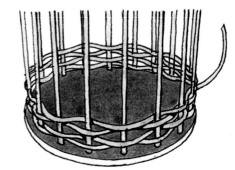

Making a basket by bending reeds in and out of the upright canes.

By overlapping the leaves and twisting them, a long continuous thread can be made. If these threads are twisted together (or *plied*) a strong rope can be made.

Alternatively, tufts of sheep's wool that were found on the ground or caught on bushes, could have been collected and spun into yarn in the same way.

Seven thousand years ago, when farming first began, people used basically the same kinds of animal hair and plant fiber that we use today.

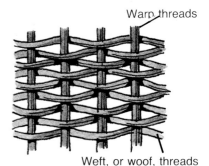

Warp threads

Weft, or woof, threads

Weaving is the same principle.

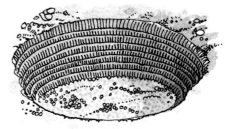

An Egyptian clay pit marked by basketwork which has since rotted away.

A suspension bridge in Peru. The many strands of rope make it very strong.

Plant Fibers

Flax

The first plant that was grown for spinning and weaving was flax, and the cloth into which it is made is known as linen. Flax is a small plant with red or blue flowers, and it is the stalks that are used to make the fibers. The stalks are soaked in water until the green part of the plant rots away (called *retting*) and the fibers are then separated and dried. The fibers are scraped to remove any pieces of wood and dirt and combed to leave the fibers straight and parallel to one another. Flax was mainly grown in Egypt where it was also used to extract linseed oil.

Hemp was the first fiber plant grown by the Chinese and is treated in much the same way as flax. It produces a much coarser fiber and was mainly used for making ropes. Other plants that produce coarse fibers for ropes, sacking, canvas, and matting are jute, ramie, hemp, sizal and coconut.

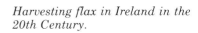

Flax.

Harvesting flax in Ireland in the 20th Century.

Cotton

The cotton plant is a member of the hollyhock family, and the first records of its cultivation come from India. The fruit, called a boll, is about an inch across and contains twenty or more seeds attached to which are long white hairs. When the fruit is ripe, the boll bursts open, forming a ball of cotton wool, called a lint. When these have been carefully picked, the cotton is separated from the hairs by beating with sticks.

Different varieties of cotton plants have evolved over the years. In India and Asia they grow as small trees with red or yellow flowers and in America as bushes 1-1½ meters (3-4½ ft) high with creamy white flowers. The finest cotton with the longest hair (or staple) is Sea Island cotton.

Cotton fruit or boll.

Animal Fibers

Silk

Silk is an animal fiber which is produced by silkworms, the caterpillars of several different species of moth which feed on the leaves of mulberry trees. Silk was first produced in China, and production of the raw material remained a monopoly of the Chinese until the early Middle Ages.

When the silkworm is ready to change into a chrysalis, it spins a cocoon around itself for protection. The silkworm, like the spider, produces a very fine thread from special glands inside the body. The silkworm squirts out liquid silk through two tiny holes beneath the mouth called *spinnerets*.

The egg-shaped cocoon has three layers, the innermost being a thin papery envelope. The next layer is the very long spun silk 450 to 1400 meters (1350-4200 ft), and its surface is hardened with gum. The outer layer, or floss, is a fluffy tangle of loose silky fibers.

After removing this outer layer, the cocoon is dropped into very hot water which dissolves the gum. The end of the silk thread is found by lightly brushing the surface, and is then wound onto a small winder. The *filament,* or thread, is so fine (like the spiders web) that threads from several cocoons are wound together to make the yarn or raw silk, and after that another twisting or *throwing* is needed to make it strong enough for weaving. In the best conditions 1kg (2.2 lbs) of caterpillars produces about 12kgs (26.4 lbs) of silk a year, and it takes two days work to reel 1kg silk by winding two or three filaments together by hand. As a result, silk has always been a very expensive luxury material.

Today, two-thirds of the world's supply of silk is produced by Japan. Any increase in this supply would require more mulberry leaves to feed the silkworms, and nearly a million Japanese farmers are already engaged in growing mulberry leaves. A lot of research has been undertaken in Japan to find a substitute food, made from soya flour, which the silkworms will eat.

Spinneret

A silkworm will eat mulberry leaves for thirty days, and molt four times before spinning its cocoon.

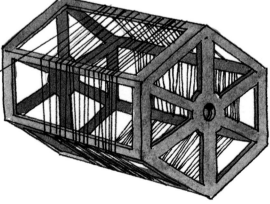

Winding silk from a cocoon onto a wooden frame. The ends of broken thread can be pressed together again, as the silk contains a natural gum.

A cocoon.

Wool

Wool is another animal fiber, which comes from the hair of sheep. Sheep were first domesticated in Mesopotamia but now live mostly in the cooler climates of the world.

The earliest sheep had fairly short wool which molted during the summer months and was probably combed or plucked by hand. Once metal scissors had been invented, the wool or *fleece* was sheared or cut off in one piece, like a coat.

The hairs from the back are the coarsest, to protect the animal from the weather, and the hairs from the belly and neck produce a softer, finer wool. Sheep in the colder climates have shorter and coarser wool and in northern countries this was usually made into *felt*.

There are many varieties of sheep all over the world, and their hairs can be short or long, straight or curly (*crimped*). Long, crimped hair is the easiest to spin.

It appears that the Egyptians considered wool unclean so it was mostly used in Mesopotamia and farther north where the colder climate stimulated a demand for warm clothing. Wool was also much easier to dye than flax so the Mesopotamians tended to wear much more brightly colored clothes than the Egyptians.

Other animals such as goats, camels, and llamas also provide hairs that can be spun and made into textiles.

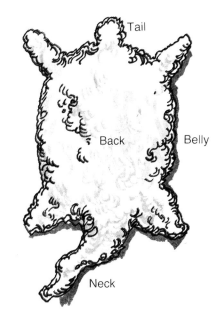

A fleece – below is a sheep being sheared with electric clippers; skilled men can shear 120 or more sheep in a day.

Black Welsh Mountain Sheep.

Romney Marsh Sheep.

Camel.

Alpaca.

Angora Goat.

9

Spinning and Weaving

To make a continuous thread suitable for weaving, animal or vegetable fibers have to be drawn out parallel and twisted together. Originally this would have been done by rubbing between the palms of the hand or between one hand and the cheek or the leg. The twisted thread was then wound onto a stick.

Later on this stick developed into a *spindle* which can be used to twist the thread. The spindle can be spun by hand, or if the spindle is weighted, it can be spun like a top. The fibers are carefully drawn out by hand and the amount of twist controlled by holding the fiber between the thumb and forefinger before letting it go to take up the twist. The *yarn* is then wound round the spindle and the operation repeated until the spindle is full.

Wool, prior to spinning, would have been pulled apart to disentangle the hairs and remove pieces of dirt. It would often have been twisted into a loose rope or *roving* and wound around a stick called a *distaff* ready for spinning.

The yarn is then made stronger by plying or twisting two or more threads together, with the twist in the opposite direction to that of the original thread.

This method of spinning is still in use in many parts of the world today and was not superseded in Europe until the 13th Century AD.

A drop spindle – having drawn out some fibers from the rolag the spindle is twisted and allowed to drop. See picture on page 3.

Rolag
Fibers drawn out
Yarn
Weight or whorl

Rolag

Spinning in Nigeria today. The woman on the right is drawing out the fibers ready for spinning.

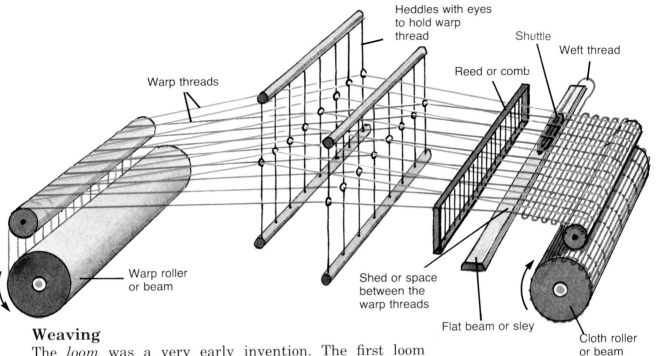

Warp threads

Heddles with eyes
to hold warp
thread

Shuttle

Weft thread

Reed or comb

Warp roller
or beam

Shed or space
between the
warp threads

Flat beam or sley

Cloth roller
or beam

Weaving

The *loom* was a very early invention. The first loom consisted of two pieces of wood pegged out on the ground with threads held taut between them. These are known as the *warp* threads.

The first weaving was probably a form of darning with a continuous *weft* thread put over and under the warp threads at right angles by hand. Then two other inventions enabled the weft to be threaded straight through. First the alternate warp threads could be raised by turning a piece of wood called a shed rod on its side. Then, every other warp thread was put through a loop attached to a rod, called a rod *heddle*. When one series of warp threads was raised, the weft thread could be passed through the gap or *shed* that was opened up. The rows of weft were then beaten tight against one another with a comb or *reed*.

Ground looms such as this are still used by Bedouins today. Vertical looms were invented quite early (about 2000 BC) and had the advantage that they enabled the weaver to sit upright. Some had weights attached to the warp threads to hold them taut.

Diagram of a loom. The heddles are raised alternately and the shuttle is slid along the sley through the gap or shed between the warp threads. The reed or comb pushes the weft yarns tight against one another.

A Bedouin woman using a horizontal ground loom, similar to that used 5000 years ago. See also illustration on page 1, showing an African upright loom in use today.

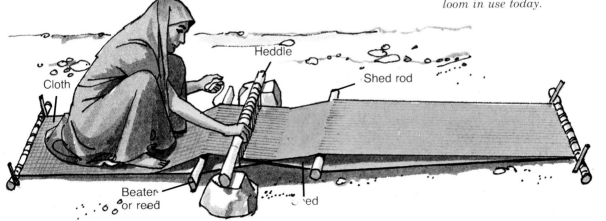

Heddle

Shed rod

Cloth

Beater
or reed

11

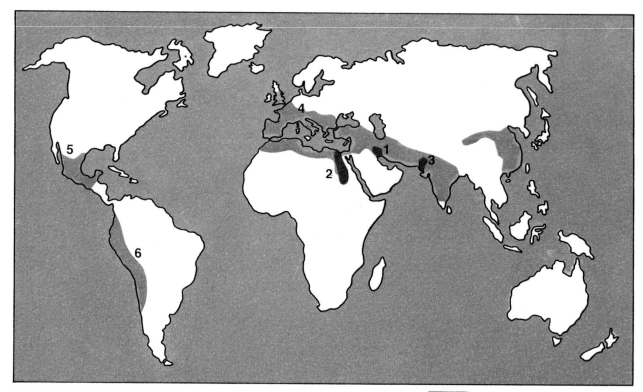

The Dawn of Civilization

By about 5000 BC, our ancestors had made two most dramatic discoveries which were to change their way of life completely; they learned how to domesticate animals and cultivate plants. For the first time, it was possible for people to abandon the nomadic life and live a settled existence in one place by growing all that was needed to feed an expanding population.

Villages, towns, and even cities, began to grow up. There was enough food to provide a surplus to support new classes of people who had time to undertake the organization that was required to run such cities, or to develop the skills of writing and mathematics. Others became specialist craftworkers.

Unfortunately, this also meant a change in the pattern of human relationships, so that primitive cooperation and sharing of work was replaced by an aggressive and competitive struggle for possessions. As a result some people became rich and others became poor.

As time went on, the clothes of the rich became more elaborate and beautiful, enabling craftsmen to design and create beautiful patterns and embroidery. The variety of clothing grew, often reflecting the great wealth of the rich, but the poorer people wore simple clothes that were cheap and more practical for working in the fields or workshops.

■ Civilizations 3000 BC

▨ Civilizations 1000 BC – AD 200

1 Western Asia
2 Egypt
3 India
4 Europe
5 Middle America
6 South America

Map of the world showing areas of the early civilizations.

The First Cities

The early farmers spun and wove their own cloth in their homes, which happens in many parts of the world today. When society became organized into towns and cities, the demand for fine clothes for the wealthy led to a flourishing trade in textiles.

At this time there arose a class of specialized craftsmen who could earn a good living with their skills, and merchant families who bought and sold the fabrics that were produced.

In Mesopotamia the craftsmen were organized into Guilds, and each different craft of spinning, weaving and dyeing was handed down from father to son. Apprenticeship to the trade was recognized by the authorities, and even the slaves who were employed in the temple workshops could become apprentices.

In Egypt the spinning and weaving was done in the towns and on the large estates by women. Later, in Europe, trade expanded and craft guilds arose in the towns where the work was mostly undertaken by men, working in small factories.

By 2000 BC patterned cloth was made by using colored weft threads and by varying the number of warp threads that were raised together. The cloth produced was so fine that the linen found in the tomb of Tutankhamen had 280 threads to the inch.

Very beautiful *tapestry* was also produced. Tapestry is woven by hand from the reverse side, the weft threads not carrying right across the warp threads but only inserted where they appear in the design. The warp threads are widely spaced and can hardly be seen. Large tapestries are usually designed to hang sideways, as the weft threads are stronger than the warp threads.

An Egyptian lady wearing a dress of fine cotton or lawn with an elaborate jeweled collar.

Warp

Weft

A tapestry picture. The colored weft thread is woven backward and forward across each part of the picture, an outline of which is pinned to the back of the wooden frame.

13

The Dark Ages

After the fall of the Greek and Roman Empires, European society changed little, and there were few scientific and technological discoveries. In Roman times slavery had divorced productive work from the wealthy classes. Men with leisure had no interest in inventing new methods of production, nor had they the incentive to do so when there was plenty of manual labor to do the work.

Europe became a continent of warring states, with power in the hands of the feudal lords and the church. The serfs on the estates of the lords and the church were better off than slaves because they led a more secure and settled existence, and were able to raise their own families. Nobody was particularly interested in changing their way of life. There was certainly little or no change in the way textiles were produced in Europe for the next 1000 years.

The Chinese had invented a silk-reeling machine in the first century BC but they kept their secret and the monopoly of silk production to themselves. Some Persian monks smuggled some silkworms out of China in 6th Century AD supposedly in a hollow cane, and a flourishing silk industry grew up in Byzantium (Constantinople). Europe did not produce silk until the 12th Century when it was introduced into Italy.

Between the fifth and tenth centuries, waterwheels were increasingly used as a source of power. In the ninth century a device called a cam, originally invented in Greek times, was coupled with the waterwheel. This was used, among other things, as a power-driven "trip" hammer in the textile trade.

A fulling mill where woolen cloth is beaten after weaving (see page 19). The trip hammers are lifted and released, hitting and sliding off the striker plate on the tappet wheel. The hammers are shaped so that the cloth is constantly turned.

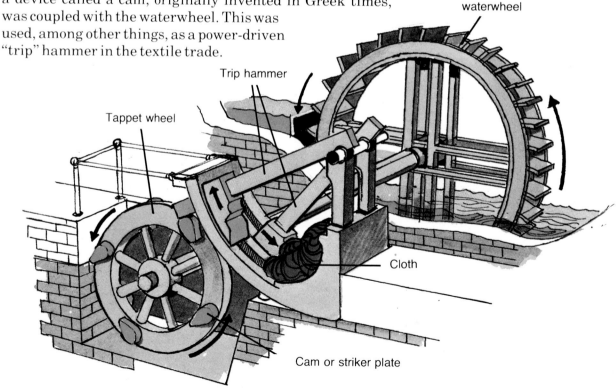

Undershot waterwheel

Trip hammer

Tappet wheel

Cloth

Cam or striker plate

The Middle Ages

The increasing use of water power in the Middle Ages led to what is sometimes known as the Medieval Industrial Revolution. This water power probably contributed more than anything else to the growth of the European economy and trade.

The first European textile factories in the Middle Ages were the silk-throwing or winding mills in Italy in the 13th Century. These were powered by undershot water wheels which allowed 2-3 operators to do the work of hundreds of hand spinners.

Flax was grown all over Europe by the Middle Ages, and continued to be the main vegetable fiber until the 18th Century. During this time the only significant invention was the flax breaker which broke up the stalks between two pieces of wood.

Cotton manufacture had been developed on a large scale by the Moors in Spain and had spread throughout Europe in the 12th and 13th Centuries. Cotton imported from Syria and Egypt was made into a coarse cloth called fustian.

Wool production provided the most important development in the textile trade. By the 15th Century many different varieties of sheep had been bred in England and there were over fifty grades of English wool. Most of the English wool was exported to Flanders, the main woolen cloth producing country at that time. English cloth was considered inferior because the wool was not sorted carefully enough before spinning.

Wool was also exported to Italy. In Florence the textile industry formed the heart of the economy and many of the rich merchants became bankers with branches in France, Flanders and London.

Wealthy Italians wore elaborate clothes made of fine wool and cotton and beautiful silk and velvets.

The simple clothes of the peasants were more comfortable for working but they would be made of coarse wool or fustian.

Weaving

In the Middle Ages the advances made in the construction of the loom made life easier for the weaver but made little difference to the speed of production. Looms had strong wooden frames and the heddles were raised by pedals or treadles. The *reed* was hung from a batten and by pressing a lever the weaver could release the warp threads from the warp beam at the back and roll the cloth onto the cloth beam at the front, resulting in a continuous process.

Spinning

The major medieval invention made in the 13th Century was the spinning wheel. This was later known as the Great Wheel or the Walking Wheel, and this more than doubled the production of the spinner. The spindle is mounted horizontally on a piece of wood and has a driving band connected to the wheel. The spinner turns the wheel in a clockwise direction with the right hand, and draws out the fibers from the rolag with her left hand, allowing them to twist, while walking away from the wheel. The spinner then holds the wool in the air and spins the wheel again so that yarn is wound onto the spindle.

The Great Wheel could be as large as 1½ meters (60 inches) across and was used in factory production for more than 200 years. The women stood in rows and worked at the wheels (which were nearly as tall as they were) and it was estimated that they could walk up to 30 miles a day backward and forward without being out of reach of their wheels.

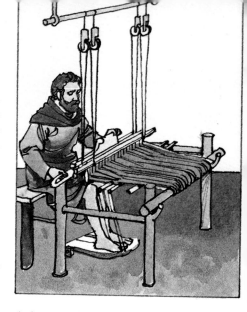

A fourteenth-century English loom. The heddles are lifted by cords connected to the foot pedals by pulleys attached to an overhead beam.

The Great Wheel. The spindle is spun by the wheel and twists the fibers. The spinner in the picture is about to wind the twisted fiber onto the spindle by holding the yarn at right angles to the spindle.

Rolag

Spindle

Driving ban

The Flyer

Before the end of the Middle Ages (15th Century) the invention of the *flyer* enabled the spinner to spin and wind the yarn onto the bobbin simultaneously. The spinner could also sit down to spin.

The Flying Wheel has the spindle mounted in a U-shaped piece of wood called the Flyer. The wool is threaded through a hole in the center of the shaft of the spindle. The *bobbin* is mounted on the spindle and is turned by a separate driving band from the wheel. The wool is passed through the hooks and wound onto the bobbin.

The Flying Wheel was never used in factory production. This was because the wheel had to be small and was therefore much slower to use, but the principle of the flyer was incorporated in the early spinning machines of Arkwright and Crompton (pages 25, 28).

The spinning wheel most commonly used today by home spinners, is turned by a pedal or treadle. This was invented in the early 16th Century. The treadle is connected by a rod or "footman" to the driving wheel, and once the wheel has been set in motion by hand, it is kept turning by the foot.

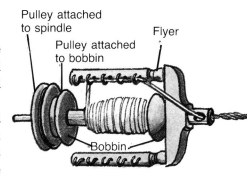

Pulley attached to spindle

Pulley attached to bobbin

Flyer

Bobbin

The flyer winds the yarn onto the bobbin by spinning faster (or slower) than the bobbin. The yarn is moved from one hook to the next as the bobbin is filled up. When it is full, the bobbin can be slipped off the spindle and replaced by another.

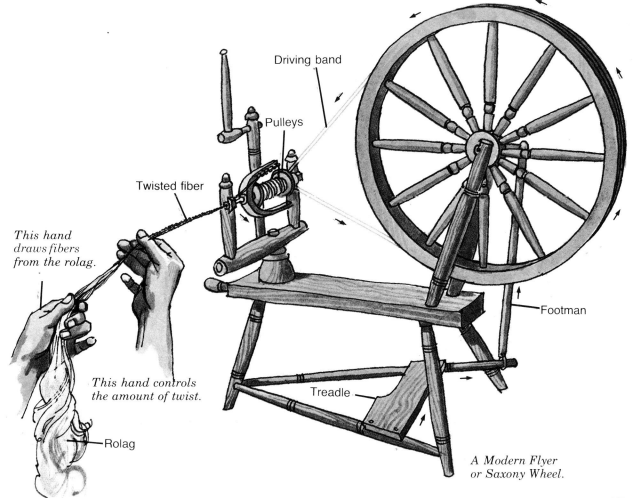

Driving band

Pulleys

Twisted fiber

This hand draws fibers from the rolag.

This hand controls the amount of twist.

Rolag

Footman

Treadle

A Modern Flyer or Saxony Wheel.

Preparation of Fibers

Disentangling woolen fibers for spinning is called *teasing*, or *carding*, and used to be done with thistle or teasle heads. The French in the 13th Century invented wire-tooth boards called carders, such as those still used by hand spinners today.

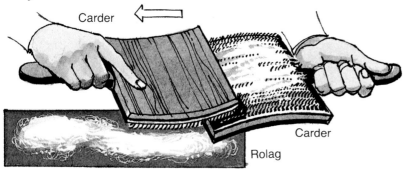

Carder

Carder

Rolag

Teasel

Carders covered with wire teeth. One is drawn across the other, separating the woolen fibers.

Combing is an alternative method which disentangles and also draws the strands of wool out parallel to one another. This idea probably derived from the linen industry

The free comb is often warmed on a stove so that it softens the natural grease in the wool and makes it easier to separate the fibers.

Comb fixed to post

Batting cotton.

where the fibers are combed with metal teeth. The advantage of this method is that it makes it easier to separate the long fibers which are more suitable for spinning fine wool. The resulting roll of wool ready for spinning is called a *roving* or *rolag*.

Wool, if it is very dirty, is washed before carding. This removes the oil or grease, which have to be replaced before spinning.

Cotton

Before carding, the cotton fibers have to be separated from the seeds. This was done by beating or batting with a stick of hazel or holly. Any dirt falls with the seeds through a grating made of cords. The dust from any of the processes in the preparation of cotton fibers is likely to cause a lung complaint called byssinosis. This has always been and still is a problem in the cotton industry.

Finishing

After cloth has been woven, it is treated, or *finished*, in various ways. It has to be washed and bleached and dyed, and possibly teased or *printed*, unless it has already been dyed before it is woven. Until 1750 cotton cloth was simply laid out on the ground to be *bleached* by the sun. First it had to be immersed in a mixture of lyes made from the ashes of trees and plants, *soured* or bleached with buttermilk and then washed by hand in the streams. It took eight months to prepare a piece of cloth in this way for dyeing.

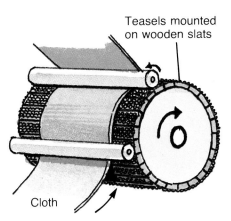

A bleachfield or croft.

Pieces of cotton cloth are laid out in the fields and bleached by the rain and sun.

Fulling

Woolen cloth requires an extra finishing process called *fulling* which makes the cloth thicker and firmer. This was done by trampling it underfoot in a trough with a mixture of fullers earth and wood ash in water. As early as 1185, water-driven mallets had replaced the use of feet, making it possible to treat several pieces of cloth at once. Trip hammers improved efficiency and encouraged the growth of the wool trade, especially in areas like Yorkshire where there was a plentiful supply of fast moving water. The use of the word "mill" for a factory is still in use in the textile industry today and derives from these early water mills. Woolen cloth was then "tentered" or hung out to dry. At the same time it was stretched along boards on which it was hung by "tenterhooks."

Gig mills for raising the *nap* on cloth like velvet were invented to replace hand teasing, and improved this particular finishing process. A roller covered with teasels was rotated in one direction, while the roller carrying the cloth rotated in the opposite direction.

Teasels mounted
on wooden slats

Cloth

In a gig mill, the surface of the cloth is roughed up by the action of the teasels.

Dyeing

Dyeing can be carried out at various stages in the preparation of cloth. In Mesopotamia it was sometimes done by dyeing the sheep before the wool was taken from the animal.

Most of the dyes that were produced were made from plants. The oldest are indigo and woad. Indigo is made from the Indigo plant which came from India, which goes blue when allowed to ferment. Woad is a plant of the cabbage family, which was grown in Europe. It is well known as a blue dye that the Ancient Britains covered themselves with to look more warlike. Madder was cultivated in Roman times and this produced a crimson dye. Yellow dyes were made from plants called weld, safflower or fustic, and green was produced by mixing these with woad or indigo. Black was produced by using a mixture of green vitriol (iron sulphate) and oak galls. Many other plant, fruit and vegetable dyes are used nowadays by home spinners to produce some very subtle and attractive colors.

The oldest animal dye was the famous Tyrian purple, used in Roman times, which was made from the shell of a mollusk called Murex. Other red dyes were made from insects, cochineal which now is used only for coloring food being the best known.

It had been known from the earliest times that cloth would take up colors more readily and intensely when treated with aluminium salts or alum known as a *mordant*.

Alum is frequently found mixed with iron which destroys its effectiveness. It is thought that alum was originally separated out by crystallization. By the 13th Century the Arabs had discovered that this could be done by boiling with urine (which contains ammonia).

If the wool or yarn is dyed before weaving, then patterned fabrics can be woven from the different colored threads. This is the origin of the phrase "dyed in the wool." Alternatively the cloth can be dyed after it is woven, or "dyed in the piece." Colored patterns on the cloth can be produced by *printing*.

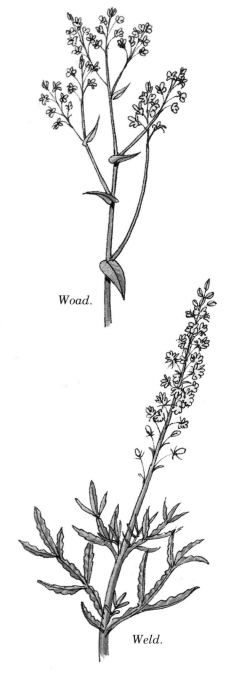

Woad.

Weld.

Blackberry.

Saffron crocus.

Onions.

Many wild plants, flowers, and fruits are used to dye homespun wool.

20

Knitting

Knitting is a different method of creating fabrics, which has the advantage of producing an elastic material. Instead of interweaving two sets of threads at right angles to one another (which produces a firm cloth) it is made from one piece of yarn, each row being looped and hanging onto the one before. Until the sixteenth century, knitting was done with a pair of knitting needles, or on a peg frame, sometimes called a Knitting Nancy.

Knitting is done using one piece of yarn.

The origin of knitting is not known, but the Arabs are thought to have produced knitted cloth in the first century AD.

The greatest demand for knitted goods was for stockings, or *hosiery*. A Nottinghamshire clergyman, William Lee, invented a stocking frame in 1589. He used a line of bearded needles, with a springy hook on the end, the machine having a presser bar to bend the hooks back against the needles. This principle is still used in knitting machines today, especially to produce fine knitting. In 1849 the latch needle was invented by Matthew Townsend. This is similar to the needle that is used in hand rugmaking and has a hinged flap which automatically closes the hook as it is withdrawn.

A Knitting Nancy – the yarn is wound around and looped over each peg in turn.

William Lee's stocking frame.

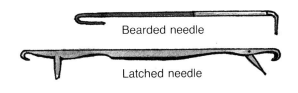

Latched and bearded needles used in knitting machines.

The Clothiers

During the 15th Century, England changed from a producer of wool to a manufacturer of cloth. This was because Flemish craftsmen who had emigrated to England and settled in East Anglia had taught their superior spinning and weaving techniques to the English. As a result the quality of cloth was greatly improved. In the Tudor period, the Spanish oppression of the Netherlands and the persecution of Protestants by the Inquisition led to an even greater influx of Flemish craftsmen.

Once the production of cloth was carried out on such a large scale for the export market, the small independent weavers had to be organized. They fell under the control of the merchant, or clothier, who bought the raw wool and handed it out in turn to the spinners, the weavers, dyers and fullers.

The clothiers made high profits, and as the industry spread to other parts of the country such as Yorkshire and Somerset, they formed the basis of a new class of industrialists with money to invest. The great merchants had much influence in the big cities such as Hull, Bristol and London, and ranked with the nobility in their wealth and power. Their wealth was politically important because they were able to provide the King with the necessary money to fight wars and to become independent of the feudal aristocracy.

The increase in trade created a big demand for gold and silver for currency. The journeys of discovery inspired by the search for gold are sometimes called the first "gold rush."

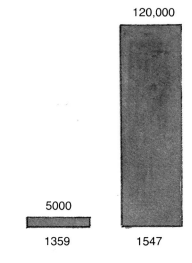

Increases in the export of pieces of cloth from Britain over 200 years.

Sailcloth is spun and woven from hemp.

The journeys of discovery – Christopher Columbus discovered America in 1492 in the Santa Maria.

Early Industrial Developments

The stimulus for further developments in the European textile industry was a combination of the increased home market (due to a rising standard of living from the time of the Renaissance) and the demand for goods created by the huge overseas market that opened up following the great geographical discoveries.

Weaving

Increased wealth and the consequent demand for luxury fabrics like damasks and figured velvets concentrated attention on the drawloom. This had come into Europe from China, where it was used to weave complicated patterns in silk, by varying the number and position of the warp threads each time the shuttle was passed through them. A harness above the loom had cords attached to the weft threads which were weighted. A "draw" boy, perched on top of the harness, would pull up the appropriate warp threads as the weaving continued. In about 1600, a French weaver devised a method of drawing the cords to one side so that by using a series of levers the boy could stand to one side of the loom.

Flying Shuttle

In 1733, John Kay patented his invention called the flying shuttle. This was a boat-shaped box containing a reel of weft thread (called a cop) which slid along a piece of wood (called a *sley*) under the lower set of warp threads. The shuttle was shot from side to side by a sharp knock with a piece of leather or wood called a picker. This was operated by pulling the cords first to one side and then the other. Kay's invention meant that not only could one weaver now do the work previously done by two, but also the width of the cloth could be twice as wide as before, when it had been limited by the span of a man's arm, about 30 inches (12 cm).

John Kay (1704–1764) started work in a woolen factory as a reed maker. Among his several inventions, he is famous for his flying shuttle. His patent was copied throughout the weaving trade, without payment and he was nearly ruined by spending all his money on taking to court people who had stolen his invention.

Weavers were afraid they would be put out of work, and in 1753, a mob broke into his house and he barely escaped with his life. He fled to France, where he died in poverty and obscurity.

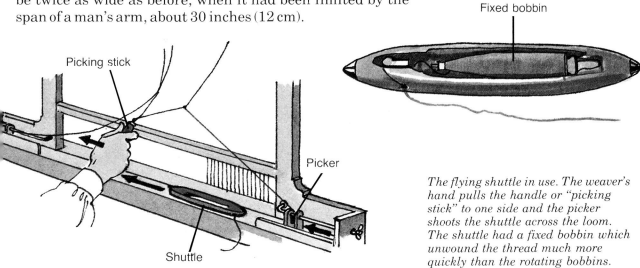

Picking stick

Picker

Shuttle

Fixed bobbin

The flying shuttle in use. The weaver's hand pulls the handle or "picking stick" to one side and the picker shoots the shuttle across the loom. The shuttle had a fixed bobbin which unwound the thread much more quickly than the rotating bobbins.

The Industrial Revolution

As in medieval times, it was largely the demands of the textile industry that speeded up the technological changes that led to the Industrial Revolution.

Despite the importance of his invention, no portrait of Hargreaves is known to exist.

Spinning Machinery

The invention of Kay's flying shuttle had meant an enormous increase in the demand for yarn (particularly cotton) to supply the looms. It was the pressure of this demand which encouraged the English inventors to develop more efficient spinning machinery.

Diagram of the spinning jenny (a picture of the jenny is on the front cover). The clasp is pulled back from A to B as the spindle is rotated by turning the wheel, and this twists the fibers. When the clasp is released and returned to A, the yarn is wound onto the bobbin and more fibers are drawn from the rovings.

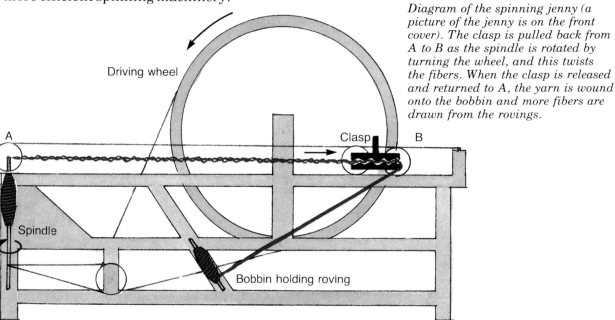

Hargreaves' Spinning Jenny

James Hargreaves from Lancashire was a handloom weaver who was also a carpenter. He is said to have watched the way a spinning wheel continued turning after it had been knocked over, which gave him the idea for the spinning jenny (jenny means engine) which he invented in 1763. He patented it in 1770.

Hargreaves' wheel drove eight, then sixteen, and later as many as a hundred spindles. The rovings were drawn out by pulling back the bar or carriage on the upper part of the frame. The wheel was then spun, putting a twist into the yarn and winding it onto the bobbins.

Even though this machine was operated by hand, and was therefore small enough to use in a cottage, it was still regarded with suspicion by workers who feared it would throw them out of work. In 1768 Hargreaves' home was attacked and twenty jennies he was building in a barn were destroyed by workers anxious to protect their livelihood.

James Hargreaves, (1720–1778) invented the spinning jenny solely for himself and his family, but it was soon in use in many homes and factories for spinning cotton. Hargreaves went into partnership with a Mr James and built his own cotton mill in Blackburn. This was not very successful, and like Kay, he spent most of his money in court proceedings against those who used his invention without payment. At the time of his death there were 20,000 hand jennies in use, with 80 spindles each. Although he did not die in poverty, his children were very poor after his death.

Lewis Paul and John Wyatt had patented an idea for machine spinning in 1738. The thread was drawn through a series of pairs of rollers, each pair spinning faster than the previous pair and with one imparting a twist, but this was unsuccessful.

Arkwright's Water-frame Spinning Machine

Richard Arkwright worked with a clockmaker named Kay. Together they invented a machine that drew out the threads with pairs of rollers and then used flyers to twist the threads. They patented the machine in 1769.

Unlike the jenny that needed three separate operations to spin and wind, Arkwright's frame had a continuous action, but could not be operated by hand. Horses were used to drive the first machines, and Arkwright built his first factory using water power from the River Derwent, near Derby.

Arkwright settled in Nottingham, and by 1788 there were 140 Arkwright water mills in operation. These almost completely replaced the large spinning wheel. Very often the strong wiry yarn from the Arkwright frame was used in weaving for the warp thread while the more elastic fiber from the jennys supplied the wefts.

Arkwright became very rich and was knighted. He was known not only as the "much inventing barber" but also as the man who gave Britain "the power of cotton."

Sir Richard Arkwright (1732–1792) was a traveling barber and wigmaker without any knowledge of spinning, weaving, mechanics or carpentry. He was, however, a thoroughly practical businessman and realized there was a demand for spinning machines. He used or adapted other people's inventions and made them commercially profitable. He also had a talent for managing factories, and met and persuaded people with money to finance him.

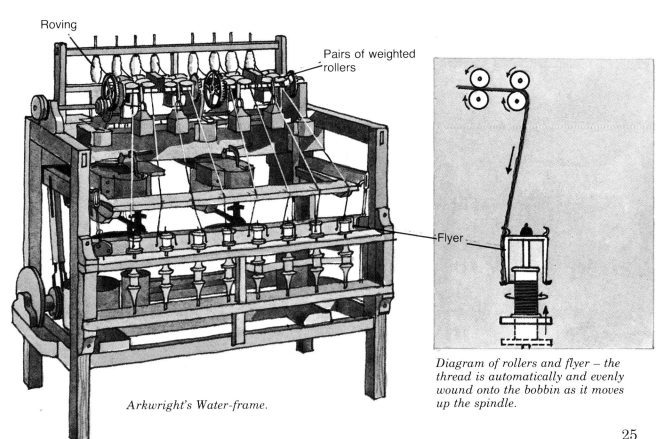

Arkwright's Water-frame.

Diagram of rollers and flyer – the thread is automatically and evenly wound onto the bobbin as it moves up the spindle.

Cotton

The cotton industry was the first to become mechanized and to use the power of steam. Being a fairly elastic yarn, cotton does not break easily, so that it was relatively easy to spin and weave on the new machines. This mechanization and cheaper cotton led to an enormous increase in the world demand for cotton.

Near the East coast of America, the plantations produced long-stapled or Sea-Island cotton, but as people moved westward in search of new land, they found they could only grow very short-stapled cotton which was much more difficult to separate from the seeds. An American, named Eli Whitney, invented a machine called a "saw-gin" (gin means engine) in 1793, which solved the problem. This had a revolving drum covered with close-set wire teeth which caught the cotton hairs. These were transferred to a second roller by brushes. This invention resulted in an increase in the output of American cotton from 250 tons a year in 1790 to 40,000 tons in 1810.

By 1861, at the outbreak of the American Civil War, the American slave plantations were producing a million tons of cotton a year. This revived the slave trade, and the number of slaves employed had increased from 700,000 in 1790 to 3,200,000 in 1850. This also increased the prosperity of towns like Manchester and Liverpool in England, which largely derived their income from the slave trade.

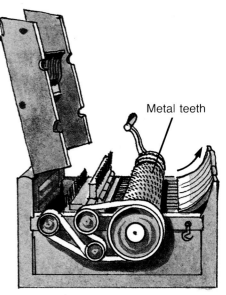

Metal teeth

Whitney's cotton gin, opened to show the metal teeth which caught the fibers and pulled them through. The seeds dropped into the box underneath.

In the course of two generations, the North of England was changed out of all recognition. In Lancashire, where there was a plentiful supply of water and coal and a damp climate more suitable to the manufacture of cotton, the population increased from 160,000 in 1700 to over 700,000 in 1800.

A slave plantation. The slaves are picking the cotton and filling the baskets under the eagle eye of the foreman.

26

Britain's "dark satanic mills."

Robert Owen (1771–1858) was a reformer who spent his life trying to change the appalling conditions of his time. The son of a Welsh shopkeeper, he started work as a boy and was manager of a Lancashire cotton mill by the age of 20.

Later, as a partner in a large mill in Scotland, he had an opportunity to put many of his ideas into practice. He reduced working hours, improved pay and conditions in the factory, built a model village with a company shop where workers could buy good, cheap food and refused to employ children under 10. He believed that "character is made by circumstance" (environment) and refused to allow any form of punishment in his schools.

The mill was so successful that he became world famous.

After 1819, he became involved in projects to set up communes first in Scotland and then in America. These unfortunately failed and he lost most of his money.

On his return to England in 1829, he devoted himself to political and social propaganda, and became the leader of the great Cooperative and Trade Union movements.

At the end of his life he lost his popularity because of his attacks on the Church, and was often regarded as a crank. His ideas were far ahead of his time, but many have now been accepted. He is regarded as the father of British Socialism.

Other industries such as mining, engineering and ironfounding grew as well, in response to the needs of the cotton industry in Lancashire and the woolen industry in Yorkshire. Towns sprang up around the mills and factories to house the workers.

The conditions in these early factories were appalling. Whole families worked in the cotton mills for long hours (up to 15 hours a day). Large numbers of children were employed because they were small enough to crawl under the machines and tie the broken ends of the threads together.

Robert Owen was largely responsible for the Factory Act of 1819 when it became illegal to employ children under the age of nine, (although children were allowed to work part-time until 1913). This was largely ignored and it was not until the Act of 1833 was passed that paid inspectors were employed to see that the law was carried out. In 1847 Parliament passed the Ten-Hours Act, reducing the working week to 55½ hours.

By 1850, although still terrible, the conditions and pay in the factories were better than any previously known. About this time approximately 1/40th of the total English population was employed in the textile industry. In 1830 the sale of cotton goods brought in half of England's export earnings. There can be no doubt that the power of cotton gave England its position as the leading industrial nation during the eighteenth and nineteenth centuries. The increase in textile production during this period meant that for the first time the poorer as well as the richer people could afford to buy healthier and more varied clothing.

Crompton's Spinning Mule

Samuel Crompton belonged to a family which, like many others in Yorkshire at this time, combined spinning and weaving with farming. He and his mother wove the flax and cotton that his two sisters spun. Between 1774 and 1779 he used a spinning jenny with eight bobbins, but finding this would not produce the warp yarns needed to weave a fine cloth, he set to work to invent a new machine.

This was called a "mule" as it combined the ideas of the Hargreaves and Arkwright machines. The thread was drawn between two pairs of rollers as in Arkwright's machine, and a moving carriage was drawn back at the same time as the rollers gave out the roving. Before the carriage was drawn back to its full extent, the rollers were stopped, and gripped the yarn, while the carriage moved back more slowly and gave more twist. The result was a very strong and fine yarn that could compete with the highest quality cotton or muslin produced in India.

The machine was designed by Crompton for domestic use and enabled the local spinners to produce these superior yarns. By 1829, 50 years after its invention, seven million out of the nine million factory spinning machines in use were modifications of the original spinning mules. By the beginning of the 20th Century, these contained 1200 or more spindles. By 1927 there were an estimated 46 million mule spindles in Britain.

Samuel Crompton (1753–1827) spent five years inventing the mule.

Such was the importance of his invention that businessmen constantly tried to steal his ideas. He eventually turned over his patent to the public, leaving other men to make their fortunes from his invention. After many attempts to raise money from the government he was given £5000 ($7500) in 1812 and a very small pension for the last three years of his life. He died a very poor and embittered man who was not appreciated until many years after his death.

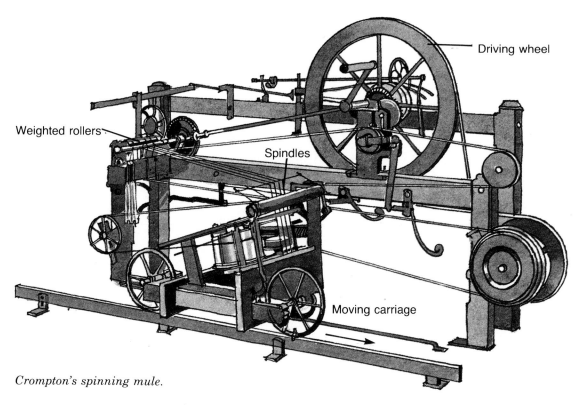

Crompton's spinning mule.

A mule factory – the man is moving the carriage by turning the wheel, the woman, or "piecer," is repairing a broken thread. The child is small enough to crawl under the machinery to pick up waste.

Spread of steam power

Before the mule could be used in factories, it had to be improved to make it more automatic. By 1800 John Kennedy had partially solved the problem, so that only moving the carriage or winding-on had to be done by hand by a skilled craftsman. In 1824, Richard Roberts, who was a machine maker, perfected a "self-acting" or fully automatic machine that was power-driven and did not require skilled workers.

The throstle was a new form of Arkwright's water-frame, which produced a stronger yarn. Where the British were more interested in improving the mule, the Americans concentrated on developing the throstle. This led them to replace the flyer with a ring.

Ring spinning

Ring spinning was invented by John Thorpe of Rhode Island in 1828. As in Arkwright's machines, the yarn is pulled through rollers, but instead of a flyer there is a small ring, or "traveler," which is dragged around the spindle. The drag of the ring causes the traveler to lag behind the spindle so that it winds the yarn onto the bobbin. In Britain ring spinning was slow to be adopted and it only became the predominant system in the 1950s.

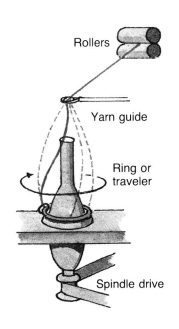

Rollers

Yarn guide

Ring or traveler

Spindle drive

Ring Spinning.

Preparation of fibers

To keep up with the demand for raw material for the new spinning machines, inventors like Arkwright worked hard to produce machines that could separate the fibers mechanically.

In 1748, David Bourn and Lewis Paul had patented a carding machine that could separate cotton or short fibers of wool. By 1785, Arkwright had developed a machine that could card cotton continuously. This used a revolving drum covered with leather in which were set millions of spiked metal teeth. Children were paid a penny for every 3000 teeth they inserted, at an average speed of 1000 a hour! The cotton was removed from the drum by a comb, and then it was passed under rollers and through a funnel, thus producing a narrow, coiled carding of cotton. It was also important to introduce machines to open up and clean the cotton. These machines used a rapidly revolving drum, with teeth inside to catch the cotton fibers, while allowing the leaves, stalks and dirt – known as "trash" – to fall to the bottom.

Wooden flats

Roving

The flax heckling machine was designed to separate flax fibers mechanically. This consisted of two sheets of combs, which moved in opposite directions.

It was the combing of wool which was the most difficult process to mechanize. The Rev. Edward Cartwright was the first to attempt this in 1792, using a revolving comb, but a more successful machine was patented in 1827.

In 1822 John Goulding of Massachusetts made a machine that combed and prepared the roving for spinning in one continuous process. At that time, the lack of skilled craftsmen in America encouraged the invention of new machinery, whereas in Britain, new machinery put the skilled man out of work. Britain had banned the export of machinery to America in 1750 in order to keep America as a dependent colony. After 1812 even skilled toolmakers were not allowed to emigrate and only managed to do so by disguising themselves as laborers or even as women.

Arkwright's carding machine. Inside the machine, wire teeth were set on the outside of a revolving drum and on the underside of the flats.

Weaving

Once spinning moved from the cottage to the factory, there was a demand for a faster, power-driven, loom. Cartwright patented his first loom in 1785. In 1787 he built an improved version, which was powered by a bull, but this was replaced two years later by steam power.

A Manchester manufacturer installed twenty-four of these machines in his factory, but this was promptly burned down by hand-loom weavers who felt that their jobs were threatened. Further attacks were made in other places, and it was not until 1850 that the use of the power loom really superseded the hand loom. Even then 50,000 of the 250,000 looms in production were still hand looms.

The main problem with the power loom was how to control the speed of the shuttle and how to make it stop automatically if the weft thread broke or the shuttle got caught in the shed. In 1840, the engineer Joseph Harrison started to manufacture superbly made looms which solved these problems. Looms of this sort were in continuous use for the next 80 or 100 years.

Jacquard loom

In weaving, the biggest advances took place in France in the silk industry. In 1801, J. M. Jacquard invented a loom that would automatically weave patterns without using a "drawboy" and by 1812, 11,000 Jacquard looms were in operation. The raising and lowering of the warp threads was controlled by cards punched with suitable holes for each row of the pattern. A perforated prism pressed against a series of needles, and only when the holes matched those in the punch card would the warp threads be raised.

At the start, the punched cards were moved by the use of a foot treadle, but by 1850 there were over 1100 power-driven Jacquard looms in Britain.

Rev. Edmund Cartwright (1743–1823) was educated at Oxford and started life as a clergyman. On vacation near Manchester, he heard from cotton manufacturers of the need for a power loom, and at the age of 40, turned inventor.

As he could not sell his idea to other businessmen, he attempted to run his own mill, but this was unsuccessful mainly due to his lack of business experience.

He moved to London in 1793, where he continued to invent, making breadmaking and brickmaking machines and agricultural implements. In 1808 he was awarded £10,000 ($15,000) by the British Parliament and bought a small farm in Kent where he spent the rest of his life.

Hooks caught on rising knife or rod

Endless belt of perforated cards

Needle into hole

Prism moves in

Needles pushed out

Connected to heddle to raise warp thread

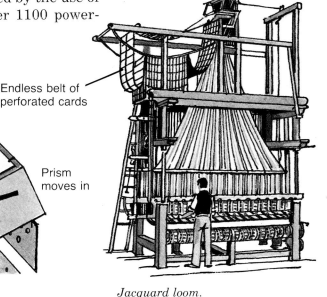

Jacquard loom.

Hosiery

Knitting had been undertaken on a fairly complicated piece of machinery, the stocking frame, since Elizabethan times. This was a hand-operated machine which was easily adaptable for power. Sir Marc Brunel invented a circular machine in 1816 that produced a tubular piece of fabric. The stockings were obviously inferior to the fully fashioned, shaped stockings made on the stocking frame. The use of Brunel's machine was vigorously opposed by the Nottinghamshire handworkers who, although they were very poorly paid, had no alternative employment.

Sewing Machine

In 1864 William Cotton invented a power-driven sewing machine which solved the problem of sewing up the stocking after it had left the machine. It was the American Isaac Singer who produced the first commercial sewing machine in 1851. A toothed plate moved the material forward at the same time as the thread in the needle caught the thread in the bobbin underneath the cloth. The machine was often worked with a foot treadle.

It was the first major domestic appliance to be sold to thousands of homes and was often paid for in monthly installments. This was the start of the system so common today. By 1860 there were 500,000 sewing machines in use in America.

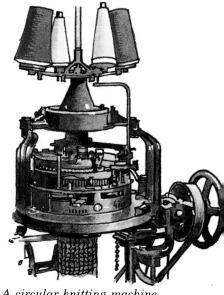

A circular knitting machine.

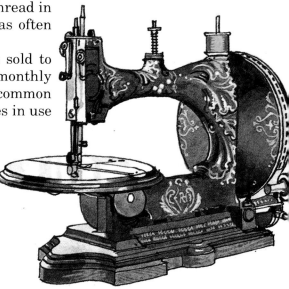

A machine made in 1870 by a London company, W.F. Thomas.

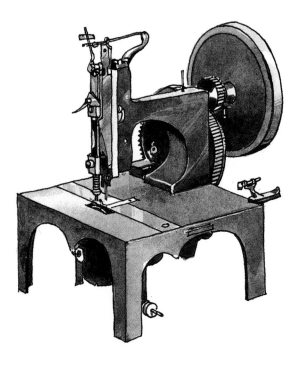

Singer's first sewing machine of 1851.

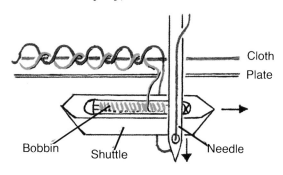

Cloth
Plate
Bobbin   Shuttle   Needle

Diagram showing how the needle catches the thread in the shuttle as it moves forward.

Industrial Developments

Compared to the inventions of new machinery for spinning and weaving in the previous 100 years, this period produced little in the way of technical changes. Most of the advances were in the preparation of fibers and in the finishing and dyeing of cloth.

Cotton

In 1850 John Mercer, an English dyer, patented a method of treating cotton with strong caustic soda. This made the fibers more elastic and enabled them to absorb dyes much more rapidly. Mercer found that this gave the cotton a luster which made it look like silk. It has been known ever since as Mercerized cotton. Unfortunately the cotton also shrank 20% in the process.

In 1895 two German dyers, R. Thomas and E. Prevost, discovered that if the mercerizing was done on a tightly stretched piece of material, it did not shrink and that the cotton had a permanent gloss. After 1895 the cheap mercerized cotton proved a powerful competitor to silk.

The Cotton Famine

In 1861, at the outbreak of the Civil War in America, the most important British industry was the manufacturing of cotton. Most of the raw material for this came from the United States; 500,000 tons a year from America compared with 100,000 tons from India.

During the Civil War the South, whose economy was based on cotton and agricultural production, was blockaded by the Union navy. The North, with its emerging industrial economy, wanted to be able to manufacture its own goods, rather than exporting the raw material and then re importing the finished goods.

The blockade, which prevented the export of raw cotton, led to an acute cotton famine in Britain. Without raw materials, mills were forced to close, and by 1863, 60% of the textile workers in Britain were unemployed. The cotton famine meant that the smaller, inefficient mills were closed down, hand weaving became obsolete, and by 1868, there were 50,000 fewer workers in the textile industry.

At the same time, the amount of cotton imported from India doubled to meet the demands of the British mills. The sudden increase in Indian cotton production had disastrous consequences for India, because vast new areas were cultivated for cotton, reducing the land available for growing food. Without land on which to grow food for themselves and their families, many peasants had to leave their villages and became homeless and landless beggars.

John Mercer (1791–1866) started work when he was nine as a bobbin tender and then learned to be a handloom weaver. He next worked in a dyeing factory, and for a short period in a printing works, before returning to weaving.

In 1813, he decided to return to the dyeing industry. He became interested in chemistry and in 1825 he went into partnership and started a dyeing business – Fort Brothers – where he remained until it was closed in 1848.

During this period he spent a great deal of time doing research and became a member of the Chemical Society in 1847. He made many very important discoveries including the composition of bleaching powder and he even anticipated Pasteur's theories about germs causing disease.

His research was recognized when he was made a Fellow of the Royal Society in 1852. He was an ardent reformer, and a generous lovable man with a practical business sense. He was not greedy and gave away the patents on his own work.

Undoubtedly, if he had been able to spend more time on research, he would have become one of Britain's greatest scientists.

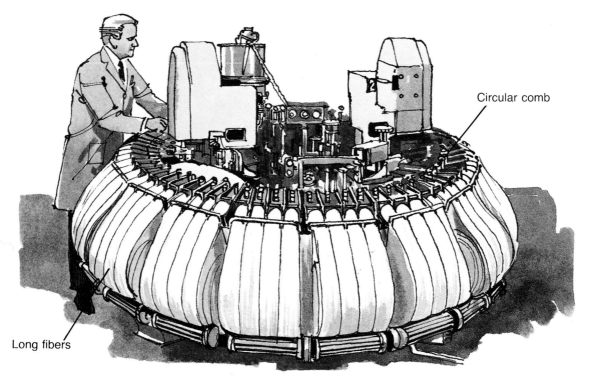

Circular comb

Long fibers

A modern version of Noble's combing machine. The comb has separated the shorter fibers and the longer ones can be seen wound up ready for spinning.

From Rags to Riches

The woolen industry in Britain was faced with the problem of competing in price with cotton. The supply of wool was increased by the use of rag-wool, called *shoddy*, made from old woolen garments. The demand for this became acute when the soldiers needed warm uniforms during the Napoleonic Wars. The main problem was to produce a machine able to tear up old cloth.

By 1830, the "rag-tearer" or "devil" was equipped with teeth. It was not until the 1850s that improved machinery, together with the treatment by acid to remove cotton fibers, was able to produce enough wool at a reasonable price.

By the 1880s, about 40% of yarn came from shoddy, and a whole new industry was created in Yorkshire. The new mill-owners in the West Riding of Yorkshire became very wealthy and "rose on rags to riches."

The wool that was produced, however, was not suitable for making *worsted* cloth. Worsted cloth is used to make suits and differs from woolen cloth, which is softer and more loosely woven. Worsted cloth requires a finer and smoother yarn, using only the long fibers lying parallel to one another, which can only be produced by combing. Usually the fibers are also carded before combing.

By 1851 machine combing was done by a machine using a series of combs on an endless belt. This solved the problem of separating the long fibers from the short and broken ones. In 1853, Noble invented a circular combing machine which is still in use today.

Weaving

Power looms for weaving, which had been far less mechanized than spinning looms, were developed in 1850. In 1895 J. H. Northrop of Massachusetts introduced the automatic loom, which was described as the loom of the twentieth century. It automatically charged the "cop" which holds the yarn, had a self-threading shuttle, and a mechanism which stopped the machine when the warp thread broke. All the operator had to do was to repair breakages, not having to handle the shuttle at all.

Northrop's automatic loom was slow to come into use in England because, apart from the opposition of the unions, it was three times more expensive than the English looms then in use. The high cost of machinery or capital equipment compared with the lower cost of labor meant that more money had to be invested in industry.

By the end of the 19th century, the United States was taking over the leadership in the invention of new machinery in the textile industry, as well as in most other branches of technology. After the Civil War, the United States had developed its own industries and was producing almost half as many cotton goods as the English.

The consumption of raw cotton in the world had quadrupled in 50 years. The price of textiles had dropped and clothes were more plentiful.

"Kissing the shuttle" or sucking the end of the thread through the eye of the shuttle. This is no longer done as it is considered unhygienic!

Weaving a plaid worsted cloth on a modern loom.

Silk and Rayon

In the mid-nineteenth century, the French silk industry was hit by a silkworm disease called pébrine. This reduced the silk production in France by about a sixth between the years 1853 and 1865. Louis Pasteur set to work to isolate the bacillus that caused the disease. This took him three years. He also pointed out that the problem was partly due to the dirty and unhygienic conditions in which the silkworms had been kept.

Another Frenchman, Count Hilaire de Chardonnet, was also investigating the silkworm disease. Observing the way the silkworm squirts out the silk through its tiny holes or spinnerets, he became interested in devising a method of doing this mechanically with other materials.

Chardonnet experimented with dissolving cotton cellulose nitrate in alcohol and ether, and forcing the mixture through fine glass tubes. The alcohol and ether evaporated, leaving a thread with a silken gloss. In 1891 he built a factory to produce the first artificial silk, but unfortunately the process proved to be explosive and production had to be abandoned.

An Englishman, Joseph Wilson Swan, was trying to develop a filament which would glow in an incandescent gas lamp by dissolving cellulose in acetic acid. His wife took the fibers and used them to spin and weave furnishing fabrics, and these he exhibited in 1885 at the London Inventions Exhibition. He had accidentally discovered another way of producing artificial silk.

In 1892, three Britons, Charles Cross, Edward Bevan, and Clayton Beadle patented the so-called viscose process for making artificial silk. Cellulose, after being mixed with caustic soda, is treated with carbon disulphide and forms a yellow-orange substance which is thinned down to a sticky syrupy mass called "viscose." The viscose is then forced through fine jets in a spinning acid bath where it solidifies into fine fibers.

A gas lamp with an incandescent mantle, usually seen in camping gas lamps today.

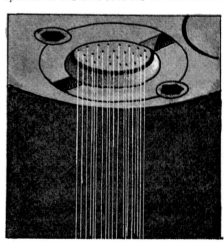

An enlarged "close-up" of a spinneret. There can be up to 16,000 holes in a spinneret 1½ cms (0.6 in) in diameter.

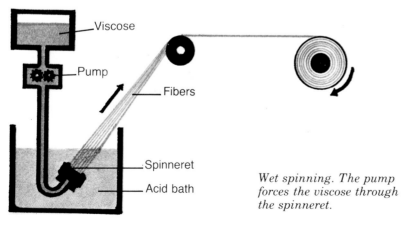

Wet spinning. The pump forces the viscose through the spinneret.

The Twentieth Century

Although methods of spinning and weaving have changed little, the production of textiles has increased enormously in the 20th Century. This is partly because of more efficient machinery but is largely due to the introduction of man-made or synthetic fibers. These contain carbon.

Carbon is an essential element contained in all living matter. The structure of the carbon atom is such that it can easily combine with other carbon atoms and atoms of other elements, to make the very complicated molecules from which all plants and animals are made.

Artificial silk or rayon is usually made from the cellulose in wood. The development of methods of manufacture took place at the beginning of the century, but it was not until after World War I that large-scale production made artificial silk cheap enough to compete with natural fibers.

The major research in the 20th Century, has been into the synthesizing of long macro-molecules of carbon from oil and coal. Coal is the compressed remains of forests of trees and plants, and oil is the product of millions of tiny sea creatures. Both were buried millions of years ago.

The research into producing synthetic fibers began in the 1930s, but strangely enough two large chemical companies on either side of the Atlantic Ocean solved the problem in different ways at exactly the same time. In 1938, representatives from E.I. Du Pont de Nemours in the U.S. walked into the offices of I.G. Farben Industrie in Germany to sell their patent for Fiber 6.6 (later known as nylon). Almost on the same day representatives of I.G. Farben walked into the U.S. offices of Du Pont with their fiber "Pe Ce."

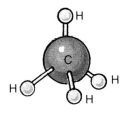

Carbon atoms (C) can combine with 4 other atoms. This is a model of methane gas with 4 hydrogen atoms (H).

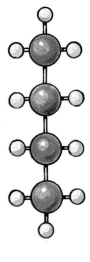

Carbon atoms joined together to form a carbon chain. This is a model of butane gas.

This is a section of a nylon molecule, which can be infinitely repeated at either end.

After spinning and stretching, the filaments can be up to 60 miles (97 km) long.

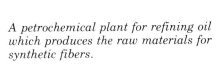

A petrochemical plant for refining oil which produces the raw materials for synthetic fibers.

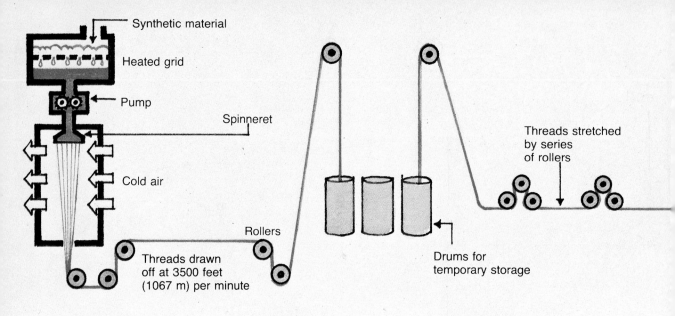

Synthetic material

Heated grid

Pump

Spinneret

Cold air

Rollers

Threads drawn
off at 3500 feet
(1067 m) per minute

Drums for
temporary storage

Threads stretched
by series
of rollers

With an outlay of 27 million dollars, Du Pont set to work to produce nylon commercially, and in May 1940 they produced four million pairs of nylon stockings which were sold within four days.

In the meantime, two British chemists, Rex Whinfield and James Dickson, were working on the use of a different chemical to produce a stronger fiber that could withstand higher temperatures. They patented the polyester fiber in 1941, but the Lancashire firm for which they were working (Calico Printers Association) could not afford the large investment to produce it. Instead the production of polyester was taken up by the large European firm, Imperial Chemical Industries (ICI). In the long run, polyester fibers have proved to be the most economically important of all the *synthetics*.

Acrylic fiber was another material that was simultaneously produced by American and German scientists, this time in 1942.

There are various methods of producing synthetic fibers, called the dry spinning, wet spinning and melt spinning processes. The word spinning is used here to describe the process of forcing the synthetic through a fine nozzle, similar to the way a silkworm or spider produces its filament. Bunches of filaments are then stretched and wound onto spools. The fibers are then cut into lengths that are suitable for spinning into yarn, and can be textured or crimped and elasticized to produce a variety of imitation natural fibers.

The recovery of the world economy after World War II and the consequent rise in the standard of living in the industrialized world allowed many more people to own automobiles. To cope with the demand for gasoline, huge oil refineries were built all over the world. In 1950, 520 million

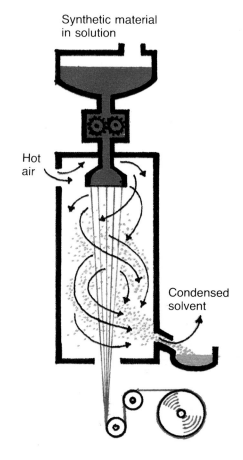

Synthetic material
in solution

Hot
air

Condensed
solvent

In the dry spinning process, hot air evaporates a solvent containing the synthetic substance. The solvent is condensed and collected for reuse.

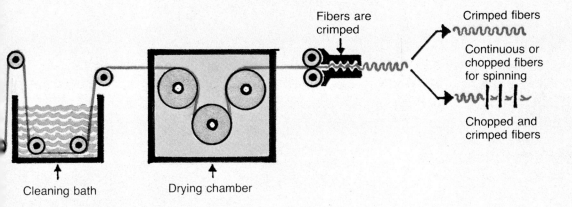

Fibers are crimped

Crimped fibers

Continuous or chopped fibers for spinning

Chopped and crimped fibers

Cleaning bath

Drying chamber

tons of oil were being produced and by 1970 this had risen to 2,500,000 million tons. This resulted in large quantities of by-products which could be used in the production of synthetic fibers, and therefore lower the price of them.

Another offshoot of the chemical industry has been the improvement in the methods of dyeing. Very bright colors can be obtained with "reactive" dyes which actually become part of the fiber molecule and have the advantage that they don't fade. With synthetic fibers, the chemical can be dyed before the filament is made so that the fibers are already colored before they are spun.

In the melt spinning process, cold air is blown onto the hot threads emerging from the spinneret, which makes them congeal into filaments.

The control room in an automated factory producing synthetic yarn. The cost of building such a factory runs to millions of dollars.

The textile industry in the industrial countries has been completely modernized. In the 1950s the ring-spinning frame became the predominant method used in Britain (as it had been for a century in America) but by the 1960s it was being replaced by "break" or "open-end" spinning machines.

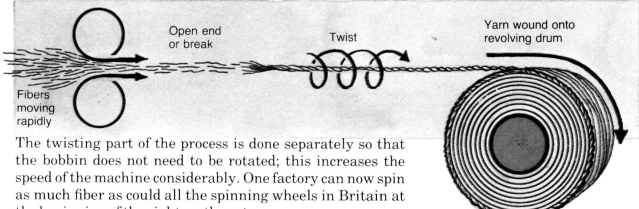

The twisting part of the process is done separately so that the bobbin does not need to be rotated; this increases the speed of the machine considerably. One factory can now spin as much fiber as could all the spinning wheels in Britain at the beginning of the eighteenth century.

Weaving has also been speeded up by using air or water jets to replace the shuttle as a method of inserting the weft yarn.

Open-end or break spinning.

At the end of the 1930s, the wool and cotton industries felt threatened by research work into the production of synthetic fibers. In 1937 the International Wool Secretariat was formed by the three major sheep-producing countries, Australia, South Africa and New Zealand. The International Wool Secretariat is now a worldwide organization which advertises the qualities of wool and encourages the sale of woolen goods. It also ensures the highest standards by controlling the quality of wool products. To help maintain quality, the Woolmark symbol was designed in 1964, and this can only be attached to new or "virgin" wool. The Woolblend symbol (1971) similarly guarantees that virgin wool forms 55% of a mixture with synthetic fibers.

No matter how much synthetic fibers are treated and crimped to resemble natural fibers, it is unlikely they will ever completely replace nature's product for clothing. The natural fibers have an elasticity and quality of insulation that comes from the structure of living cells and tissues.

Wool can absorb up to a third of its own weight in moisture without feeling wet; in fact it gives out heat when it gets wet. Cotton has the advantage of absorbing water, which makes it more comfortable for garments worn next to the skin. On the other hand synthetic fibers are cheaper to produce, they are hard-wearing, are much easier to wash and require little or no ironing. Many fabrics are produced nowadays that are mixtures of natural and synthetic fibers, in order to combine the qualities of both.

Woolmark symbol.

Woolblend symbol.

Now and the Future

There is no doubt that the advances in science and technology applied to the textile industry mean that nobody in the modern world need go short of clothes. Over the last 30 years, world production of textiles has tripled, and over half the fibers used are synthetic. In the industrial parts of the world, the amount of money people have to spend on clothes has more than doubled. With reasonable prices, many people can now afford the luxuries once confined to a few. Fashions used to be a sign of the social status of the wearer, but nowadays people can dress to please themselves.

The same is not true of the underdeveloped parts of the world, where there is not the capital to invest in modern industry. In countries like India, a lot of weaving and spinning is still done by hand and new machinery could throw thousands of people out of work, increasing the amount of unemployment and poverty that already exists.

The affluent societies too have their problems. Every few years there is an overproduction of goods. In the 1930s coffee was burned in Brazil; today there is a surplus of grain in the U.S. What happens? Without buyers, industries don't make profits and businesses go bankrupt. There is vast unemployment, and people do not have the money to buy the goods that are produced. There is also a limit to the number of things, like refrigerators or automobiles, that are actually required.

With the technology that is now available to mankind, people all over the world should be able to live in comfort. If we didn't waste money on armaments and wars, if the economy of the world was planned on a large enough scale so that the wealthy nations helped the poorer ones, if everyone instead of a few were given an adequate education (for leisure as well as work), mankind could use its knowledge and resources to provide plenty for everyone. Perhaps then we could live together in a civilized way, enjoying cooperative human relationships.

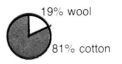

World production in 1910: 389 million tons.

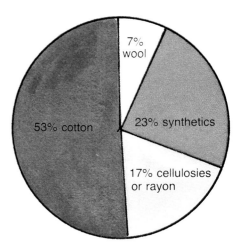

World production in 1970: 22 million tons. The percentage of synthetics compared to natural fibers is increasing every year.

Is it better to spend money on food and clothes or war and armaments?

Time Chart   5000–00BC

9000 BC	Stone age (Neolithic man)	Baskets and ropes made
		4000 BC First looms
3000 BC	Sumerian City States (Mesopotamia)	
	2613-2160 Egypt – Old Kingdom	First textile factories
2500 BC	India – Indus civilization	
	2040-1632 Egypt – Middle Kingdom	Vertical looms invented
2000 BC	Crete – Minoan civilization	
	1700 China – Shang Dynasty	
	1567-1069 Egypt – New Kingdom	
1500 BC		
1000 BC		
	Assyrian Empire	
	Middle and South American civilizations	
	524 Buddha	
500 BC	Greece – Classical civilization	
	Byzantine Empire	
	250 Roman Empire	
	220 Great Wall of China built	
		Silk-reeling machines in China
00 BC	Birth of Christ	

Time Chart   AD 300-1500

AD 300

391 Library at Alexandria burned

AD 500 Europe overrun by barbarians

Spinning wheel in India

Silk production in Byzantium (Istanbul)

AD 700 Moors (Arabs) conquer Spain

742-814 Charlemagne
849-899 Alfred the Great
        (first English King)

AD 900

Cotton and silk production established
by Moors in Spain

Wire-toothed carders in use

1066 Norman conquest of Britain

AD 1100   1095 First Crusade

Flyer attached to reeling machine in China

Spinning wheel in Europe

1206 Ghenghis Khan invades China
1215 Magna Carta

Silk-throwing mills in Italy
Trip hammer for fulling cloth

1271-75 Marco Polo's travels in China

AD 1300   Ottoman Empire

Italian Renaissance

Gig mills
Four-heddle loom
Spinning wheel with flyer

1453 Fall of Constantinople
1492 Columbus discovers America

AD 1500

1523 Spanish conquest of South America

1589 William Lee – Stocking frame

1600 East India Company formed
1620 Pilgrim Fathers, Mayflower voyage
1641-1645 English Civil War

1660 Silk-throwing mills in France

AD 1700

Time Chart   1700-1840

1700

1707 Act of Union between England and
    Scotland to form Great Britain

1720

1718 Lombes silk throwing mill

1724 Missionaries expelled from China

1733 John Kay – Flying shuttle

1740

"Age of Enlightenment" in Europe
(1694-1778 Voltaire; 1712-78 Rousseau)

1757 British victories in India (Plassey)
1760 1759 and Canada (Quebec)

1763 Hargreaves – Spinning jenny

1768 Cook's first voyage to the Pacific

1769 Arkwright – Water frame

1779 Crompton – Spinning mule

1780 1776-83 American Revolution

1788 Colonization of Australia begun
1789 French Revolution

1785 Arkwright – Carding machine
1787 Cartwright – Power loom in factories

1793 Whitney – Cotton gin

1800 1799-1815 Napoleonic Wars

1801 Jacquard – loom

1811-20 Regency period in Britain

1815 Battle of Waterloo

1815 Danforth – Throstle

1820

1822 John Goulding – Combing machine

1828 J. Thorpe – Ring spinning

1833 Emancipation of slaves
    in British Empire

1840 1837-1901 Victorian Era in Britain

Time Chart   1840-1980

Britain	America

	Britain / America
1840	1840 Colonization of New Zealand begins
	1849 Matthew Townsend – latch needle
	1850 Mercerized cotton
	1848 Revolutions in Europe
	1848 California Gold Rush
	1851 Singer – Sewing machine
	1853 Noble – circular combing machine
1860	1861-65 American Civil War
	1863 Emancipation Proclamation abolishing slavery in the United States
	1870 Franco-Prussian War
	1876 Queen Victoria created Empress of India
1880	
	1884 Chardonnet – Artificial silk
	1892 Cross, Bevan, Clayton – Viscose process
	1895 Northrop – Automatic loom
1900	1899-1902 South African or Boer War
	1914-18 World War I
	1917 Russian Revolution
1920	
	1929 Wall Street Crash
	1937 International Wool Secretariat
1940	1939-45 World War II
	1939 Carruthers – Nylon
	1941 Whinfield, Dickson – Polyester fiber
	1949 Chinese Revolution
1960	
	Break or open-end spinning
	1969 First landing on the Moon
	1964 Woolmark symbol
1980	

Glossary

Bleaching – process of whitening fabric before dyeing, normally done by using a chemical called bleaching powder (chloride of lime).

Bobbin – a reel on which thread or yarn is wound.

Carders – a pair of wooden bats, the insides of which are covered with wire teeth or hooks.

Carding – the process of separating fibers before spinning by means of teasels, carders or carding machines.

Combing – the separating and laying of fibers into parallel strands using two combs. This process sorts into short and long fibers.

Crimp – the wave or curl in a wool fiber.

Distaff – a stick on which is wound the *roving* of fibers ready to be spun.

Dye – any substance used to color yarn or cloth. It can be of natural (animal or plant) origin or from chemicals usually obtained from coal tar.

Dyeing – the process of coloring fibers, yarn or fabric.

Fabric – any cloth made from yarn by weaving, knitting or felting.

Felt – a matted fabric made by pressing fibers together.

Fiber – any hair, filament or plant material used for spinning into yarn.

Filament – a very fine thread from a silkworm or a long artificial fiber.

Finishing – processes after fabric has been woven such as bleaching, fulling, dyeing, printing or raising the *nap*.

Fleece – the wool that is cut off of a sheep in one piece like a coat.

Flyer – a U-shaped mounting on the spindle of a spinning machine which, as it twists the thread, winds it onto the bobbin.

Fulling – the thickening or felting of woolen cloth by beating and shrinking.

Heddle or Heald – the frame on a loom that carries and raises the weft threads.

Hosiery – knitted stockings.

Jacquard Loom – a loom used for weaving complicated patterns (with many changes of the warp thread).

Knitting – a method of producing an elastic fabric from one piece of yarn.

Loom – a piece of equipment used to make cloth, with warp and weft threads interwoven at right angles to one another.

Mordant – a chemical used in dyeing to make fibers absorb color more readily.

Nap – the raised fibers of velvet or similar cloth.

Ply – a number of threads twisted together to form a yarn.

Plying – the twisting together of threads to form a yarn.

Printing – the process of producing a colored pattern on a plain piece of cloth, traditionally by hand using wood blocks or a silkscreen. Most cloth is now printed in a continuous roll on high-speed machines.

Reed – a comb-like device on a loom for beating the weft threads into place, and spacing the warp threads evenly across the cloth.

Retting – the preparation of flax for spinning by soaking the plant stems in water until the green tissue rots away, (leaving the fiber).

Rolag – a long, round bundle (hank) of wool fibers ready for spinning.

Roving – loosely twisted fibers ready for spinning.

Shearing – cutting the wool off of a sheep in one piece.

Shed – the gap on a loom between two sets of warp threads through which the *shuttle* passes.

Shoddy – rag-wool made by shredding old woolen garments.

Shuttle – a stick or box carrying weft threads through the shed of raised warp threads on a loom.

Sley – the base on which the shuttle slides.

Spindle – a weighted stick used to spin wool.

Spinneret – a tiny hole beneath the mouth of a silkworm, or the nozzle through which synthetic material is forced when producing synthetic fibers.

Spinning – any method used to twist fibers into yarn, or the process of forcing liquid through a fine hole or nozzle, as used in making synthetic fibers.

Souring – a process of bleaching clothes, originally done by exposing cloth to sunlight.

Synthetics – "manmade" fibers forcing a substance made by chemical reactions through a fine nozzle.

Tapestry – a pattern or picture, often a decorative hanging, made by weaving weft threads into a fixed warp (not to be confused with embroidery, as in the Bayeux Tapestry).

Teasing – the separation of fibers before spinning which was once done with the head of a teasel plant (see also *carding*).

Thread – a fine strand, filament or fiber.

Throwing – the process of twisting raw silk to make a strong yarn.

Warp – threads that are wound onto a loom before weaving. They run lengthwise down the cloth.

Weaving – making cloth on a rigid frame or loom by passing weft threads over and under warp threads.

Weft – the threads that pass over and under the warp threads when weaving.

Whorl – the weight attached to a spindle, made from wood or stone but weighted according to the fiber being spun.

Worsted – a strong fine, tightly twisted yarn made from combed, long-stapled wool; a cloth made from this yarn.

Yarn – a continuous twisted strand of natural or synthetic fibers.

Index